In loving memory of my Father, Henry,

A child of God, a guardian to many, and a precious father.

## Acknowledgments

Writing this book has been a deeply personal and transformative journey, and I am profoundly grateful to all those who have played a part in bringing this story to life. It is with immense appreciation and heartfelt gratitude that I acknowledge the following individuals and groups:

**My Family:** Thank you for being my constant source of inspiration, my reason for pressing forward, and my greatest achievement in life. You are my world, and I dedicate this book to you with all my love.

**My Father:** This book is a tribute to my beloved Father, Henry, whose life and legacy continue to shape my perspective on courage, dedication, and service to others. Your memory lives on in these pages.

**My Mother:** To my beloved Mother, Remedios, whose resilience and love have sustained our family through all challenges, I owe a debt of gratitude that words cannot express. Your unwavering support and sacrifice have made this journey possible.

**My Siblings:** To Riza, Carina and Paul who shared the joys and burdens of our family's experiences, thank you for your love and understanding. You are the living embodiment of our shared history.

**Friends and Supporters:** I extend my heartfelt thanks to my friends and supporters who have offered encouragement, feedback, and a shoulder to lean on throughout this writing process. Your belief in this project has been invaluable.

**Readers**: To all those who will pick up this book and embark on this emotional journey with me, I am grateful for your curiosity and open hearts. It is my hope that this story resonates with you and leaves a lasting impression.

**Those Who Serve**: To all the individuals who, like my Father, dedicate their lives to serving their countries and communities, you are the unsung heroes of our world. Your sacrifices and commitments inspire us all.

Thank you to each and every one of you for being a part of this journey. Your contributions, support, and love have transformed this story into a reality, and for that, I am forever grateful.

With heartfelt thanks,
Elaine

# Chapter 1

The Promise of Pinatubo: A Journey of
Resilience and Compassion

In 1991, the Philippines, bathed in tender sunlight, resembled a serene tapestry, its colors of daily life vividly interwoven. Families moved through their routines in a timeless rhythm, children's laughter punctuating the air like music, while the sun draped its warm, comforting cloak over the land's lush contours. Here was a realm celebrated for its arresting beauty, a jewel cradled in Southeast Asia's embrace.

Yet, beneath this picturesque serenity, an ancient titan stirred in its sleep. Mount Pinatubo, shrouded in myth and mist, harbored a fiery heart within its tranquil facade. Unknown to the world, it simmered with a primordial wrath, poised to shatter the deceptive calm.

When Pinatubo awoke, it did so with an apocalyptic fury that defied belief. As if mourning their imminent demise, the azure skies curdled into an ominous grey. Titanic plumes, dense with ash and wrath, clawed their way heavenward, obscuring the sun. The land writhed under the onslaught of seismic tremors, spewing rivers of molten rage that scarred its verdant face.

Villages, once alive with activity, now lay smothered under a heavy blanket of ash and despair. Ancient structures crumbled like sandcastles, their fragments scattered by the wind. Fields that had danced with crops lay still, blanketed in a deathly pallor, transforming a once vibrant tapestry into a monochrome of desolation.

Beyond the physical ruin lay the deeper, more painful carnage — the human cost. Families were fragmented, their bonds strained and broken. Livelihoods, nurtured over generations, vanished in an instant. Communities, once tight-knit, found themselves adrift on tides of sorrow. The eruption had not merely unleashed a natural cataclysm; it had birthed an ocean of suffering, boundless and profound.

Against this backdrop of turmoil, our narrative unfolds. The characters within these pages, while products of fiction, are sculpted with the essence of the Filipino soul — resilient, compassionate, and unyielding. They are the phoenixes rising from Pinatubo's ashes, their stories weaving through the tapestry of 1991, a testament to human spirit and hope.

While Mount Pinatubo's eruption serves as a dark canvas, it's the vivid strokes of our characters' lives that bring color to this tale. They are the heart of this journey, their sagas an homage to the indomitable spirit that defines the human condition.

As you turn these pages, let the resilience of the Filipino people, the strength of their communities, and the unwavering power of hope guide you. 'The Promise of Pinatubo: A Journey of Resilience and Compassion' isn't just a story; it's a tribute to the heroes, both real and imagined, who faced down the tempest and rose anew.

# Chapter 2

## The Day the Sky Darkened

Reflecting on those events from my childhood, the memories of June 14, 1991, remain remarkably vivid, etched in my mind like a photograph in an old family album. I was just six years old at the time, and yet the emotions and sensations of that day are as fresh as if they happened yesterday.

It was a seemingly ordinary Wednesday, and I was happily fascinated in a small pocket book my mother had given me as a giveaway from a powdered milk purchase earlier that day. Our daily routine was disrupted by the arrival of my uncles, who lived nearby. They came seeking news of my father and any updates he might have had about Mount Pinatubo. Curiosity and concern drew our entire neighbourhood out of their homes, where we gazed at the colossal plume of smoke rising steadily towards the sun. Little did we know that this was the prelude to a catastrophic event that would reshape our lives.

The days and nights that followed were filled with the eerie atmosphere of power outages and trembling earth. I can still recall the sensation of being gently rocked in my bed during the earthquakes, a feeling akin to floating in a pool of water. Our nights were punctuated by hushed conversations among our neighbours, as we all grappled with the uncertainty and shared our worries and speculations.

June 15, 1991, marked a significant shift. The town was rocked by major earthquakes, and at that young age, I felt the genuine fear and apprehension that gripped us all. On that fateful day, my father chose to stay with us, understanding the potential need for an emergency evacuation. My brother's illness added to the tension; he was suffering from a severe chest infection exacerbated by the volcanic ash that blanketed our town.

My father, renowned for his dedication to serving the country, had a remarkable talent for forming deep connections with people from all walks of life. Whether it was the waiter at a restaurant or the owner of a local business, he had an innate ability to leave a lasting impression. It seemed that upon meeting him for the first time, one couldn't help but want to keep him as a friend.

In the critical hours leading up to the volcanic eruption that would devastate our town, my father's friend Boni, a construction worker, arrived with his dump truck. His timely presence was a lifeline, a testament to the strong bonds my father had forged throughout his life, and it symbolized the strength of the community that rallied together in our time of need.

As we embarked on that journey from our home to a temporary shelter, I, at that young age, didn't fully comprehend the gravity of the situation. I was more entranced by the experience of riding atop a dump truck, oblivious to the turmoil surrounding us as people evacuated, clutching their cherished belongings.

# Chapter 3

## A Prayerful Journey of Protection and Hope

The following day, as we continued to stay at the temporary shelter, my Father had to part from us. Duty called, and he was determined to lend a helping hand in the mission to save lives. Little did he know that what started as a routine assignment for search and rescue would soon become the defining chapter of his life.

With his uniform on and a heartfelt goodbye to his family, my Father set off on a journey that held unimaginable challenges. The aftermath of the eruption had left communities in ruins, and chaos reigned supreme. It was amidst this chaos that Efren's life was destined to undergo a profound and unexpected transformation.

Sometimes, life's most remarkable transformations unfold when we least expect them. Whether they stem from anticipated events or, as in Efren's case, emerge from the steady guidance of unwavering faith that permeates our daily routines, there exists an intricate dance of destiny in every moment we experience. Efren, a man who had been raised as a devout Catholic, stood as living proof of this phenomenon. His life, from its inception to its culmination, was underscored by the resonance of heartfelt prayers—a rhythm that seemed to connect with the universe, drawing people, events, and circumstances that would ultimately mold his extraordinary journey.

My father's solid devotion to his faith was a constant presence in his life. It was a faith that fortified his spirit, gave him purpose, and infused his actions with compassion. Every day, he would begin and end with heartfelt prayers, an unbroken cycle that mirrored the rise and fall of the sun. Within the sanctuary of those sacred moments, he would commune with a higher power, seeking guidance and strength.

On that fateful day, as he embarked on his mission, I am certain that his prayer was a simple yet reflective one—a conversation between a devoted servant and his Creator. "God," he must have whispered, "I am your child, and I am your servant. Watch over me as you shape me into an instrument of protection for the many who need it."

In that prayer, my father affirmed his commitment to a higher purpose. He understood that his role in this world transcended the ordinary, that he was meant to be a protector of the vulnerable and a beacon of hope in times of darkness. His faith had endowed him with the firm belief that, guided by divine grace, he could make a difference in the lives of those who had lost their way.

As we reflect on his journey, we come to realize that faith, in all its forms, has the power to shape our destinies in selfless ways. It becomes the cornerstone upon which we build our lives, providing strength when we face adversity and direction when we stand at crossroads. It connects us to a larger purpose, one that extends beyond our individual aspirations and resonates with the needs of our fellow human beings.

My father's life stands as a testament to the reflective interplay between faith and destiny. It serves as a reminder that, even in the face of unexpected challenges, unwavering faith can be a guiding light, illuminating the path toward a greater calling. It is a force that attracts positivity, inspires compassion, and transforms ordinary individuals into instruments of change.

In the pages of this story, we witness how faith shapes destiny, how the rhythm of prayers can harmonize with the universe, and how one man's constant belief in a higher purpose can lead to an extraordinary journey of protection, compassion, and hope.

# Chapter 4

The Triumph of the Human Spirit:
Unearthing Strength in Vulnerability

While on duty, fate led Efren into the hands of the most wanted rebel group in the country. Mistaken for a threat due to his uniform, he found himself shackled and captive under the watchful eyes of the group's leaders. Coincidentally, the rebel's family was also trapped in their home, which had already been ravaged by destruction, and they were unable to leave due to their son had been a high-priority target even before the eruption began. The first few days were filled with uncertainty and fear, with Efren's heart pounding in his chest as he pondered his fate.

As days turned into nights within the battered confines of the rebel leader's home, Efren asked the rebel leader, "Why do you fight?" The leader replied, "For the same reason you wear that uniform – to protect what we love.". Their discussion sent shivers down his spine as he realized their intentions to recruit children as soldiers, innocent young souls thrust into the heart of conflict. This revelation struck him like a bolt of lightning. His thoughts raced back to his own children waiting for him back home, their laughter, their dreams, and the life he had always envisioned for them.

One evening, as the moon cast a soft glow over filtering through the damaged walls, Efren found himself engaged in a heartfelt conversation with a young child named Elena. She was no older than his own children, and her eyes carried the weight of someone who had witnessed far too much too soon. Elena shared her dreams of a better life for her family, her voice trembling with a mixture of hope and despair.

Efren listened attentively, the fate of his own family weighing heavily on his mind. In that vulnerable moment, their shared dreams and aspirations bridged the gap between captor and captive. The bond they forged transcended the confines of their situation, and Efren came to realize that even in the direst of circumstances, there existed a glimmer of humanity.

Elena's words lingered in Efren's mind long after their conversation had ended. Her dreams became his inspiration, and a promise began to take shape within him. He understood that should the day of his liberation come, he would dedicate himself entirely to guiding the rebels towards a more peaceful course and safeguarding the innocence of young souls, just like Elena.

This newfound determination became his guiding light, a beacon of hope amidst the darkness of captivity. It was a promise he intended to keep, for Elena, and for all those whose lives were touched by the chaos of conflict.

*In the crucible of vulnerability and the darkest of circumstances, the human spirit often reveals its most profound and awe-inspiring power. It's a testament to the resilience, adaptability, and innate strength that reside within each of us.*

*Resilience Amidst Adversity:*
When life takes an unexpected turn, and individuals find themselves at their most vulnerable, it's astonishing to witness the human spirit's capacity to bounce back. Whether it's coping with a debilitating illness, recovering from a traumatic experience, or facing personal losses, our spirit can become a wellspring of resilience. It's a reminder that even when the world feels like it's crumbling, our inner strength can help us rebuild.

*Empathy and Compassion Shine Brightest:*
Darkness often brings out the brightest sparks of empathy and compassion. In the face of personal adversity, individuals often discover a profound understanding of the suffering of others. This empathy can drive them to reach out, support, and uplift others who are also navigating their own trials. It's during our most vulnerable moments that we connect with the vulnerability of others, forging bonds that transcend our individual challenges.

*Finding Purpose and Meaning:*
When life's circumstances seem overwhelmingly bleak, many people discover an uncharted sense of purpose and meaning. It's as if adversity acts as a crucible, refining our values and clarifying our priorities. Individuals often

emerge from their darkest moments with a profound sense of purpose, driven by an inner calling to make a positive impact, not just for themselves but for the greater good.

*Courage in the Face of Fear:*
The human spirit's ability to summon courage when facing fear is nothing short of remarkable. Whether it's standing up against injustice, confronting personal demons, or facing the unknown, the power of the human spirit allows individuals to move forward despite their fears. This courage can be a guiding light through even the most daunting of journeys.

*Transformation and Growth:*
Adversity has the unique ability to spark personal growth and transformation. When individuals find themselves in their darkest moments, they often embark on a journey of self-discovery. They confront their limitations, challenge their assumptions, and emerge from the ordeal as stronger, wiser, and more resilient versions of themselves. It's a testament to the human spirit's relentless pursuit of growth and self-improvement.

*Inspiration for Others:*
The power of the human spirit, when displayed in the face of vulnerability and adversity, serves as an inspiration to others. It becomes a beacon of hope, a reminder that even in the direst circumstances, one can find the strength to endure, to overcome, and to thrive. The stories of individuals who have triumphed over darkness often inspire and uplift countless others, creating a ripple effect of resilience and positivity.

In summary, the power of the human spirit in times of vulnerability and darkness is a testament to the indomitable nature of the human soul. It reminds us that even when we are at our most fragile, we possess an inner strength that can overcome the most formidable challenges life throws our way. It's a power that resides within each of us, waiting to be discovered and harnessed when we need it most.

# Chapter 5

## Lost in the Night

On that day, when my Father said his goodbye, it marked the beginning of the longest and most agonizing nights I had ever endured, a memory that continues to haunt me even now. The temporary shelter we occupied was already brimming with people who had lost their livelihoods and loved ones. Amidst this sea of sorrow, my Mother couldn't help but be consumed by worry for my Father.

She clung to the radio unit he had left behind for communication during his mission. It was her lifeline to him, the only thread connecting her to his whereabouts and well-being. In those unrestrained times, all telephone lines lay shattered, rendering them incapable for gathering information.

Days stretched into an eternity, each one devoid of news from my Father. As the second day dawned without any word from him, my Mother's anxiety reached a breaking point. She took matters into her own hands, rushing to the nearby police station and calling upon our family friends who served in the military. Desperation fueled her plea for assistance in locating her beloved husband.

In the depths of that poignant moment, I confronted a deep and unexpected sorrow that often eludes children at the tender age of six. My Father had always been my hero, a towering figure whose presence dominated my world. Yet, in an instant, that comforting certainty was shattered, replaced by a sense of loss that I couldn't fully comprehend.

Our lives were swallowed by worry, and each night felt like an eternity, punctuated by the haunting echoes of tearful moments. It was a childhood interrupted, disrupted by circumstances beyond my control. At the age when I was just beginning to embrace school and form friendships, my reality was abruptly transformed into something I couldn't have foreseen. The cruellest twist was the cloud of uncertainty that hung over my Father's fate, a constant reminder that I might never see him again.

Amidst the chaos of emotions that enveloped our family, I grappled with my own turmoil. It was a solitary struggle, one that I wasn't prepared for. Should I mirror my Mother's tears or wear the same worried expression as my sister and brother? The weight of my Father's absence pressed heavily on my young shoulders. I yearned for his return, yet, absurdly, I remained trapped within the confines of my own emotions, unable to articulate the storm that raged inside me.

The vulnerability of children during times of catastrophe, conflict, or war is a stark and sobering reality. These young souls, often unable to fully articulate their emotions at such a tender age, bear the brunt of circumstances beyond their control. My own experience serves as a reminder of just how fragile a child's world can become in an instant.

At the age of six, I stood on the precipice of newfound independence, eagerly taking my first steps toward the realization of dreams that glittered on the horizon. The simple joys of attending school, sharing laughter with friends, and the promise of a bright future were abruptly overshadowed by the relentless tide of uncertainty that swept over my life.

The eruption of Mount Pinatubo shattered the tranquillity of our existence, and I found myself grappling with a reality I was ill-prepared to comprehend. The abrupt disruption of my routines, the fear that gripped my heart, and the knowledge that my father, my hero, might not return, all cast a long shadow over my once-innocent world.

For a child, it's a jarring awakening to the harsh realities of life. The sudden disruption of normalcy forces you to confront emotions and fears that seem far too weighty for your fragile shoulders. There's an overwhelming sense of helplessness, an inability to make sense of a world turned upside down.

In those trying times, my dreams and aspirations became casualties of circumstance. The uncertainty of whether I would ever attend school again, see my friends, or, most poignantly, reunite with my father, cast a pall over my young heart. It was a struggle to navigate the tumultuous sea of emotions that raged within me.

Yet, amidst the chaos and uncertainty, the resilience of childhood innocence perseveres. Despite the hardships and disruptions, children have an innate ability to adapt, to find moments of joy even in the darkest of times. The laughter of friends, the warmth of family, and the simple pleasures of life continue to provide solace and hope.

Reflecting on those challenging days, I am reminded of the importance of nurturing and protecting the well-being of children during times of crisis. Their vulnerability is a call to action for communities and societies to ensure their safety, emotional support, and the preservation of their dreams. It's a testament to the indomitable spirit of children, who, despite the odds, manage to find resilience and hope even in the face of adversity.

# Chapter 6

## Caught in the crossfire

As Efren's release drew near, destiny charted an unforeseen course. A military unit, on a mission to locate him, inadvertently ventured into the vicinity of the group's devastated home. This encounter escalated into a confrontation, and Efren became ensnared in the midst of a fierce firefight. The ensuing exchange of gunfire left him marked with indelible scars, both physical and emotional.

In those harrowing moments, as searing pain coursed through his body, Efren clung desperately to the cherished memories of his family. It was their faces, their love, and the unspoken promise he had made to them that provided him with the strength to bear the turmoil surrounding him.

Leaving the hospital with a metal implant in his left leg was a daunting new beginning for Efren. He faced the formidable challenge of reconstructing a life irrevocably altered by the scars of his past. The struggle to accept his newfound physical limitations weighed heavily on him, a constant reminder of the sacrifices he had made.

Efren's journey paralleled the resilience of the Filipino people who, too, had been tested by the cataclysmic eruption of Mount Pinatubo. The eruption, which occurred on June 15, 1991, was one of the most powerful volcanic eruptions in the 20th century. It led to the displacement of hundreds of thousands of Filipinos, resulted in over 800 casualties, and caused widespread devastation.

Yet, in the face of such devastation, the Filipino spirit remained unbroken. The people of the affected communities rallied together with unwavering resolve. They embarked on a collective journey of rebuilding their lives and their beloved land. Homes were reconstructed, communities were revitalized, and the scars of the disaster gradually faded into the background.

The resilience of the Filipino people served as a beacon of hope, a testament to the human spirit's ability to rise from the ashes. Despite the daunting challenges and immense losses, they chose to stand strong, rebuild, and look toward a brighter future.

In the aftermath of Mount Pinatubo's eruption, the world witnessed a remarkable display of unity, courage, and determination. The scars on both the land and its people were reminders of the past, but they also told a story of resilience, rebirth, and the unyielding spirit of a nation that refused to be defeated by the forces of nature.

# Chapter 7

## Unveiling Resilience and Letting Go

While composing Chapter Six: Caught in the Crossfire, I discovered myself grappling with a profound blend of emotions that gripped my heart. Writing about my Father's unwavering commitment to serving our country was no simple endeavour, as the gravity of his dedication had been a burden I had borne for so long.

My Father's love for his fellow countrymen and his tireless devotion to their well-being left me in awe. His life was a testament to the ideals of citizenship and service, qualities that seemed to flow through his veins. As I penned those words, I couldn't help but feel a swell of pride for the man who had shown me the true meaning of **selflessness**.

But it was also on this page that tears welled up in my eyes, as vivid memories of visiting my Father during times of illness came rushing back. I was faced with an image of him that I had never anticipated in my life—a version of him weakened by health struggles. Those moments had been heart-wrenching, a stark contrast to the strong and vibrant presence I had always associated with him.

As I continued to write, I confronted a truth that had long been buried within me—an anger that had simmered beneath the surface. I had resented his passing, a feeling that had gnawed at me for years. I couldn't help but think that if only he had taken better care of his health, if only he hadn't dedicated the majority of his life to serving our countrymen, he might still be with us. The weight of that anger had been a heavy burden to bear.

But as the words flowed onto the page, I felt a cathartic release. It was as though the act of writing had allowed me to acknowledge and process my anger, ultimately leading to a sense of acceptance and forgiveness. I came to realize that my Father's commitment to service was an integral part of who he was, and it was a legacy worth celebrating, not resenting.

In the pages of this book, I found closure, and I let go of the anger that had held me captive for so long. I came to understand that while my Father's physical presence may be gone, his love and the lessons he imparted would forever shape my life. As a daughter, I would always need my father, and his memory would continue to guide me on my own journey, reminding me of the importance of service, love, and forgiveness.

# Chapter 8

## A Scent of Resilience

In the shadow of the once raging Mount Pinatubo, my childhood town of Porac lay blanketed in a thick coat of ash. The streets where I once played tag were now silent, gray pathways. I was six, holding Mama's hand tightly as we walked through this unfamiliar world, trying to make sense of the changed landscape that was once so full of life and laughter.

Despite the devastation, there was a pulse of activity. The Kapampangan people, my people, were everywhere, clearing debris, rebuilding, their faces set with a determination that seemed to defy the very mountain that had altered their lives. They moved like a dance of resilience, a dance I was too young to join but old enough to understand.

As we passed the churches and chapels, I saw groups of people working together to repair what the eruption had tried to erase. The sounds of their tools were like a strange music, a hymn of hope and strength. I would watch, wide-eyed, feeling a mix of awe and a strange sadness as I clutched a doll - the only thing I had managed to save from our home.

Our house, or what was left of it, stood quietly in the midst of the destruction. I remember stepping over the threshold, the scent of ash and lost memories heavy in the air. The walls that once heard my giggles now stood silent, listening to the soft sobs of my mother. I didn't fully understand the loss, but I felt it—a deep, aching sadness that was too big for my little heart.

But even in the midst of such sorrow, there was a moment of unexpected joy. One evening, drawn by the delicious smell of cooking, we found ourselves at a neighbor's house. They were preparing a feast of Kapampangan dishes, each one a celebration of survival and tradition. As I took a bite of the tangy, sizzling 'sisig', I was transported back to a time before the ash, before the fear. It tasted like home, like safety, like hope.

Around the table, people shared stories of loss but also of courage and new beginnings. I listened, not always understanding, but feeling a bond forming, a shared strength. These stories, these people, they were weaving a tapestry of resilience, and I was a part of it, even at six.

That night, as I lay looking up at the stars, the same stars that shone above both our old world and this new, altered one, I felt a deep sense of connection. The stars whispered of a vast, unchanging universe, and I realized that even in the face of great change, some things remained constant, comforting.

As dawn broke, painting the sky with promises of a new day, I felt something shift inside me. Inspired by the unyielding spirit of my people, I made a silent vow. I didn't know what the future held, but I knew I wanted to be a part of this story of healing and hope. I understood, even then, that from the heart of disaster, we had not only found the scent of survival but the flavor of a future being reborn.

# Chapter 9

## Echoes of Resilience: Navigating the Unknown

I have vivid memories of the meals our family shared in the aftermath of the eruption. It was a time when the term "relief goods" reverberated throughout our town, offering a glimmer of hope in the darkest of hours. These relief packages, filled with food and essential supplies, were generously provided by the government and various organizations. Their arrival was always announced by the unmistakable sound of a dump truck's siren, a welcome signal that help was on its way.

In those days, our temporary shelter seemed like an immense cave to my six-year-old eyes, filled with the echoes of numerous families and the perpetual hum of conversations. It was a colossal space, where laughter mingled with the soft murmur of voices, creating a symphony of resilience. The shelter, crowded and vast, was both overwhelming and fascinating to me.

During those challenging days, my mother engaged in heartwarming exchanges with our neighbours. We would trade items from our relief packages if we had a surplus of something. Though I longed for the specific flavors of home, the shared meals here had a taste of solidarity, a shared understanding that we were all in this together, navigating a new world where the ground beneath our feet was a canvas of muddy footprints, each telling a tale of survival and hope.

We were filled with questions, but time seemed to slip through our fingers, and everyone yearned to return to their homes and rebuild their lives. Tragically, our town was struck by yet another disaster: two powerful tropical cyclones that targeted the very area where the eruption had inflicted its initial damage. These storms dispersed the volcanic ashfall far and wide, wreaking havoc on our crops.

During this tumultuous period, I also learned about the term "lahar," a volcanic mudflow even more treacherous than lava flows. Amidst conversations about the aftermath, I held onto the burning desire to return home. I also longed for my school supplies, which still had that new stationery scent since I had only just begun attending school before the eruption.

Then came the news about my father, who had been rushed to the hospital, fighting for his life. We were informed that we could all stay in the hospital while my father underwent surgery and recovered. It was during this time that I felt utterly adrift. The transition from the temporary shelter to a hospital was a situation I, as a young child, couldn't fully grasp. I began to question whether this kind of devastation, one after another, was a normal part of every child's life. Would my father ever walk again? What kind of life lay ahead for me after all of this, and when would the relentless cycle of disasters finally cease.

As I lay in the hospital, waiting for my father's recovery, I yearned for the promise of a new day. I hoped that someday, I would wake up and realize that all of this – the eruptions, the cyclones, the temporary shelter – had been nothing more than a nightmarish dream. In my heart, I clung to the hope of returning to a life where the wonders of my imagination were the only adventures I needed to face.

Reflecting on that turbulent chapter of my life, I am struck by the profound impact that the eruption of Mount Pinatubo had on my family and me. It was a time when the very essence of our existence was put to the test, and the bonds of community and resilience were forged in the crucible of adversity.

The arrival of relief goods, accompanied by the blaring siren of the dump truck, is a sound etched into my memory. Those packages represented a lifeline, a glimmer of hope amid the chaos. It was during this period that I witnessed the beauty of solidarity as my mother selflessly shared with our neighbours, teaching me the importance of generosity in times of need.

As a young child, the eruption shattered the semblance of a carefree life I had known. I could no longer make simple requests for my favorite meals, and our temporary shelter became a haven for bewildered children like me, all grappling with the enormity of the situation. The questions that filled my young mind were unending, and I wondered if this level of devastation was a common thread in the lives of children everywhere.

The subsequent onslaught of tropical cyclones and the menacing specter of "lahar" challenged us further, testing our resilience and resolve. Nature seemed relentless in its trials, yet the desire to return to our home, our haven, remained a constant ache in our hearts.

The news of my father's hospitalization cast a shadow of uncertainty over our lives. The shift from our temporary shelter to the hospital was disorienting, and I found myself struggling to comprehend the gravity of the situation. I questioned the fairness of it all, yearning for a return to the familiar and the comfort of routine.

In hindsight, that period was marked by turmoil, fear, and longing for stability. It was a time when the world felt unpredictable and unrelenting, yet it also revealed the strength of the human spirit and the resilience of the Filipino people. It instilled in me a profound appreciation for the value of home, family, and the unwavering human spirit in the face of insurmountable challenges.

These experiences have deeply influenced the person I've become, constantly underscoring the significance of empathy, community, and treasuring those moments of tranquillity and normalcy that we often overlook. As I pen down these thoughts, I can't help but feel a lump in my throat. Even in my thirties, I sometimes find myself yearning for the comforting presence of my parents, a sense of security that transcends age.

The yearning for my childhood home, as it once stood, tugs at my heartstrings with an enduring pull. Despite the trials and tribulations, we endured, it remained a sanctuary within my soul—a testament to my roots and the crucible that shaped the person I've become today.

Moreover, as I reflect on my journey from childhood to adulthood, I've come to appreciate the depth of my experiences. I've witnessed and endured much since my early years, and now, as an adult, I find value in those formative circumstances. In my homeland, where children typically enjoy carefree lives, we possess a remarkable resilience. Whether facing natural disasters or times of conflict, the indomitable spirit and unwavering positivity of my fellow citizens inspire hope and promise for a brighter future.

# Chapter 10

## Amidst the Ashes

In the small, ash-covered home that once bustled with life, Maria and her daughter, Ella, sat in a corner untouched by the pervasive gray dust. The air was heavy with the scent of sulfur, a constant reminder of the destruction wrought by Mount Pinatubo. Despite the efforts to clean up, traces of the eruption lingered everywhere, settling into the cracks and gaps like unwanted memories.

Ella asked, "Mama, will we be okay?" Maria, with a reassuring smile, responded, "We've always found a way, haven't we?". "Mama, will things ever be the same again? Our home, Papa, everything feels so broken."

Maria, her hands still from trying to wipe away the persistent ash, took Ella's face in her hands, her touch gentle. "My dear, after such a disaster, things may never be exactly the same. But that doesn't mean we can't rebuild, can't find happiness and strength again. Look around; yes, there's ash, there's damage, but there's also us, together, unbroken."

Ella's eyes scanned the room, the grey dust almost like a blanket over their once vibrant home. "But Papa, he's coming back different, hurt. How do we help him when everything is so... so changed?"

Maria's voice was steady, a rock in the midst of chaos. "Ella, your father is indeed coming back with scars, with pain that's not just physical. But remember, we are his home, his comfort. Just as we'll clean away the ash from our home, we'll help clear the pain from his heart."

She paused, her gaze settling on a picture frame, the glass cracked but the family photo still smiling through. "This eruption, it's taken so much from us, but it hasn't taken our spirit, our love for each other. Like our people, who've already started to clean, to rebuild, we too will rise from this. Our family, our love, it's stronger than any eruption, any tragedy."

Ella leaned into her mother, seeking comfort in her presence. "I'm scared, Mama. Scared for Papa, for us."

Maria wrapped her arms around her daughter, the two of them in a small town of hope amidst the grey. "It's okay to be scared, my child. But never lose hope. Your father, he's a fighter, and with us by his side, he'll find his way back. And just think of how far you've come, the kindness and compassion you show every day. You're the light in this darkness, Ella. You and your siblings, you're the reason we'll get through this."

As they sat together, the house silent but for the distant sounds of the community beginning to stir, to clean, to rebuild, Maria and Ella found strength in their bond. They were a family, a unit, tested but not defeated. And in that moment, amidst the ash and the memories of devastation, they knew they would rise again, stronger and more united than ever before.

# Chapter 11

## Profound Insights and Renewed Understanding

As my Father was no longer able to participate in the routine military service trainings due to his injuries, his expertise as a criminal profiler did not go unnoticed. The head of the military unit recognized his valuable skills and promoted him to the position of Chief of the Criminal Investigation Unit.

Efren's unwavering faith had always guided his daily routines. It was the cornerstone of his life, setting the tone for his actions and decisions. As he assumed the role of Chief of the Criminal Investigation Unit, his faith in humanity remained unshaken.

Efren believed that every moment held the potential for transformation and redemption. This deep faith fueled his determination to make a difference in the lives of juvenile offenders.

A juvenile offender asks, "Why do you care?" Efren replies, "Because someone once cared for me. It's time I paid that forward." He knew that by providing these young souls with a chance for rehabilitation and support, they could break free from the cycle of violence and crime.

Efren's faith and his commitment to empathy and compassion became a driving force for positive change. He understood that by instilling hope and offering a second chance, he could create a brighter future for the children caught in the crossfire of conflict and adversity.

His remarkable transformation from a soldier to a protector of the most vulnerable serves as a poignant reminder that life's journey is a profound and often unpredictable odyssey. It underscores the long-lasting power of the human spirit to find purpose and understanding in the unlikeliest of circumstances.

He was a living testament to the resilience of the human soul, a testament to the idea that even in the face of adversity, we have the capacity to evolve, to transcend our roles, and to embrace a higher calling. When Efren first embarked on his military career, he could not have fathomed the path that awaited him—a path fraught with challenges, unexpected detours, and profound revelations.

In the tumultuous currents of life, it's easy to feel lost, adrift in a sea of uncertainty. But it's during these moments, when the world seems most chaotic, that the seeds of purpose can take root. It's often when we face unexpected challenges and navigate uncharted territory that we discover our true calling.

The path to finding one's purpose is seldom linear or predictable. It may involve unexpected detours, setbacks, and moments of doubt. Yet, it's precisely these experiences that shape us, molding our character and refining our values. They force us to confront our strengths and weaknesses, helping us understand who we are at our core.

How we react to the chaos and unpredictability of life is what sets the course for our journey. It's in those crucial moments of decision, when we choose resilience over despair, hope over defeat, and purpose over aimlessness, that we begin to shape not only our own destiny but also the world around us.

Our reaction to adversity ripples outward, impacting those we encounter along the way. When we find our purpose amidst the chaos, our actions become a source of inspiration and empowerment for others. We become beacons of hope, reminding those around us that they too can navigate the storm and emerge stronger, wiser, and more determined.

In the end, finding your purpose amidst life's unpredictability is not just a personal quest—it's a gift you offer to the world. It's a testament to the human spirit's capacity to transform challenges into opportunities and to create positive change in the lives of others. It is a profound reminder that, even in the midst of chaos, we have the power to shape our own destiny and make a lasting impact on the world.

# Chapter 12

## The Concept of Healing

As I delved deeper into my father's legacy and the work he had undertaken during his tenure in the military, I stumbled upon a trove of handwritten notes that chronicled his research journey. His passion for justice and compassion for the vulnerable had driven him to focus a significant portion of his efforts on juvenile cases, particularly those children traumatized by conflict or victims of substance abuse.

In the pages of his meticulously kept notes, I discovered a notable shift in perspective that my father had championed—a shift from "rehabilitation" to "healing." It was a change in terminology that he believed could make all the difference in the lives of these young souls scarred by conflict and violence.

### The Power of Words

My father understood that words carried immense weight, especially in the realm of recovery for a child . He recognized that the term "healing" held a unique resonance in our culture, one that encompassed not just physical and psychological recovery but also spiritual and emotional well-being.

### A Holistic Approach

"Healing" suggested a more holistic approach to recovery. It implied a process that extended beyond the physical realm and reached into the emotional, psychological, and social aspects of a person's well-being. For a child who had endured unspeakable trauma, this comprehensive care was essential.

*Positivity and Empowerment*

While "rehabilitation" could sometimes carry a clinical or corrective connotation, "healing" exuded positivity and empowerment. It focused on growth and recovery rather than fixing something perceived as broken.

*Community Involvement*

"Healing" implied a community-driven process where support systems like family, friends, and community groups played a crucial role. This aligned seamlessly with our Filipino value of "Bayanihan," emphasizing communal unity and working together for a common good.

*Reducing Stigma*

My father was acutely aware that the term "rehabilitation" might inadvertently stigmatize these children, hinting at past wrongdoing or deviance. "Healing" reframed their experiences, focusing on recovery from victimization and trauma, which could help reduce stigma.

*Emphasis on Recovery and Growth*

"Healing" suggested a journey towards wholeness and wellness, a transformative process that allowed for personal growth and development. This was especially crucial for children who had had their childhoods disrupted by conflict.

*Alignment with Local Beliefs and Practices*

In a country steeped in traditional beliefs and practices that emphasized the importance of healing in all aspects— body, mind, and spirit—my father's choice of terminology aligned perfectly. Using the term "healing" resonated with our cultural values and could be more effective in engaging local communities in the recovery process.

In conclusion, my father's choice to adopt the term "healing" over "rehabilitation" signified far more than a mere linguistic adjustment; it marked a deep shift in perspective. "Healing" encapsulated the holistic and community-driven approach essential for the recovery of children traumatized by conflict. It symbolized hope, growth, and an unwavering dedication to guiding these children toward a brighter future.

# Chapter 13

## Embracing the New Beginning

Alas, life was slowly stitching itself back into a semblance of normalcy. As the days unwound, they brought with them a familiar yet distant routine. Schools, once closed doors amidst the chaos, began to beckon us back. I remember that morning vividly, the sky a canvas of soft blues and the sun, a gentle golden orb, peering curiously at a world reshaping itself.

For me, a child whose world had been upended, the reopening of schools was a vessel of mixed emotions. Excitement fluttered in my heart at the thought of seeing friends, of learning, of partaking in the innocent joys of childhood once more. But beneath that excitement was a tether of reluctance, a subtle yet persistent pull towards the safety of my family. The past month, though shadowed by tragedy, had been an unexpected gift of time with them. Leaving their side now, even for the haven of school, felt like an unspoken goodbye to a chapter of closeness we might never relive.

In school, the air buzzed with the energy of reunited friends and stories eagerly shared. But amidst the laughter and chatter, a new routine took shape – one that the eruption had etched into our reality. Earthquake drills became as commonplace as morning assemblies. We practiced them with a seriousness that belied our tender years, a reflection of the lessons etched into our young minds by the rumbling earth and ash-laden skies.

These drills, though a stark reminder of our changed world, also imbued in us a sense of preparedness, a feeling of being equipped to face whatever lay ahead. I learned then that resilience was not just about withstanding the storm, but also about learning to dance in the rain, to find strength in vulnerability.

During this time, I was nudged, gently yet firmly, towards the threshold of a new beginning. The world beckoned, a world that had transformed in the blink of an eye. The innocence of my childhood was now interlaced with the wisdom born from facing adversity. I realized that life, much like the lahar-laden landscapes around us, was a mosaic of change and constancy, loss and discovery, fear and courage.

Embracing this new life in the aftermath of the eruption was not a choice but a necessity. And so, with a heart both heavy and hopeful, I stepped forward. Each day was a journey, each challenge a stepping stone. I was learning to embrace not just the new life, but also the new me – a child of the eruption, a bearer of stories, a seeker of light in the midst of shadows.

In this crucible of transformation, my family remained my anchor. Their love and support were the winds beneath my wings, urging me to soar even when the skies seemed clouded. Together, we navigated this new world, our bonds strengthened by the trials we had weathered.

And as the sun set each day, painting the sky in hues of resilience and hope, I knew that we, the children of Pinatubo, were blooming amidst the ashes, our spirits undimmed, our resolve unbroken. For in the heart of every end lies the promise of a new beginning.

# Chapter 14

## Echoes of Resilience: Promises and Goodbyes

In the quiet stillness of the small, dimly lit room, Ella whispers, "I'm not ready to let you go." Her father squeezes her hand, "I'll always be with you, in every step you take, in every dream you chase." The room was filled with the soft, steady beeps of machines and the faint, comforting scent of her father's cologne. His once robust frame was now frail, yet his eyes, bright and full of love, focused intently on her.

"Ella, my dear," he began, his voice a whisper, yet clear and filled with emotion, "I've watched you grow, faced challenges and triumphs with the grace and strength that only someone with a heart as big as yours could show."

Ella squeezed his hand, tears brimming in her eyes. "Dad, please don't talk like this. You're going to be okay."

He smiled, a tender, knowing smile that spoke of love and an unspoken understanding. "Ella, my time here may be drawing to a close, but I need you to know how deeply I believe in you. You're going to have a bright future, my girl. No matter what trials come your way, you'll carry on, just as we've done as a family."

Ella bit her lip, trying to hold back the tears. "But Dad, I don't know if I can do it without you."

"You can, and you will," he insisted gently. "You were raised in a family where love knows no bounds. That love, it's a part of you, Ella. It's your strength, your compass. Remember all we've been through, the challenges we've faced, the resilience we've shown. You're a part of that legacy."

Ella nodded, a single tear escaping down her cheek. "I just wish we had more time."

"Ah, my dear," he sighed, a note of sorrow in his voice, "so do I. But remember, time doesn't diminish love or the lessons learned. I may not be here in person, but I'll always be with you, in the love we share, in the memories we've created."

He paused, gathering his strength. "I want you to promise me something. Promise me you'll live fully, love deeply, and face each day with the courage and kindness that I've seen in you since the day you were born."

Ella nodded, her voice a mere whisper. "I promise, Dad."

"And know this," he continued, "I am immeasurably proud of you. Proud of the person you've become and the journey you're yet to embark on. You have so much to offer the world, Ella. Never doubt that."

As they sat together, the world outside fading away, father and daughter shared a moment of profound connection. Words were no longer necessary; the love they shared filled the room, a powerful, unbreakable bond that would endure long after his departure from this world.

And in that moment, Ella understood. Her father's love and lessons would be her guiding light, a beacon of hope and strength as she navigated the path ahead. His spirit, his love, would live on within her, today, tomorrow, and for all the days to come.

# Chapter 15

## A Father's Silent Battle

Eight years had elapsed since my father's departure from this world. He had consistently embodied robust health, a fervent sports enthusiast, graced with an unwavering set of resilient genes. Fate had cast an unusual hand for him, sparing him from the common ailments that had afflicted generations of his family.

However, life, as we often discover, can be full of unexpected turns. My father's health took a detour not due to hereditary ailments but as a consequence of his selfless service during a time of conflict. A metal implant in his leg, a silent witness to the battles he had fought, proved to be a silent adversary.

As the years marched on, that metal implant began to whisper its discomfort in the form of persistent pain. To silence the ever-present ache, my father turned to painkillers, seeking respite from the relentless agony that emanated from his leg. Little did he know that this choice, meant to alleviate his suffering, would sow the seeds of his eventual demise.

The toll these painkillers took on his kidneys was insidious, their silent erosion of his health unfolding in the shadows. It was a cruel irony that a man who had conquered adversity on the battlefield would be brought low by the very remedy he sought for his pain.

Yet, even as his health waned, my father never allowed his spirit to dim. He remained a constant presence in the lives of his family, a pillar of strength and love. His commitment to us was unwavering, a testament to his enduring presence, even as the shadow of illness loomed.

His dedication extended beyond our family's borders, reaching out to the broader community he served. In helping others, he found a profound sense of purpose and fulfilment. His life was not just about existing; it was about making a difference.

In the narrative of my father's life, I find a powerful lesson. It's a reminder that sacrifices are often unseen, that the battles fought behind closed doors can be as fierce as those on the battlefield. My father's legacy teaches us that even in the face of unexpected challenges and sacrifices, we have the power to leave an indelible mark on the lives of others. His story is a testament to the enduring strength of the human spirit and the enduring impact of a life lived with unwavering dedication and love.

In memory's embrace, my father dear,
A source of love, forever near.
With wisdom's touch and laughter's grace,
In your embrace, we found our place.

You wore your strength, a silent cloak,
Through life's challenges, you never broke.
In every moment, you stood so tall,
A guiding light through every squall.

A protector, guardian, unwavering and true,
In times of need, we turned to you.
Your love, a beacon, forever bright,
Illuminating even the darkest night.

Though you've journeyed to realms unknown,
In our hearts, your love has grown.
Your legacy lives on, a cherished part,
A testament to love's enduring art.

Through your example, we've learned to be,
Strong, compassionate, and ever free.
In your memory, we find the way,
To live with love, come what may.

So, in these words, we honor you,
A father's love, forever true.
In the story of our lives, you'll remain,
A source of inspiration, a guiding flame.
-your daughter

# Chapter 16

## A Legacy of Hope

In the gentle embrace of memory, my father's legacy continues to shine as a radiant beacon in our lives. His incredible journey from a dedicated soldier to a steadfast protector of the vulnerable has etched itself indelibly into the core of our hearts and within the very fabric of our community.

Our community, once marred by the shadow of conflict and despair, has undergone an insightful transformation. Yet, it wasn't just my father's actions that brought about this change; it was the far-reaching ripple effect of his unwavering compassion and tireless dedication. The children he so fiercely endeavoured to shield from the perils of war now stand on the cliff of a brighter future, their dreams no longer obscured by the looming spectre of violence.

The cycle of despair and hopelessness, which had gripped our community for far too long, has been shattered into countless fragments, each one a testament to the power of hope and the boundless potential that resides within each child. In place of despair, a new cycle has emerged, one that weaves together threads of hope and possibility into a tapestry of resilience.

In the tapestry of my father's life, I see the meaningful lesson that even when life takes us down uncharted and unforeseen paths, we possess the remarkable capacity to unearth our purpose and discover the profound depths of understanding. My father's legacy serves as a poignant reminder that sacrifices, though often hidden from view, can cast a lasting and transformative light upon the lives of others.

As we gaze back upon the chapters of my father's remarkable journey, we are not simply reminded of his extraordinary story. We are, above all, inspired to continue his legacy, to assume the role of guardians for the vulnerable, and to live our lives with an unwavering commitment to love and compassion.

My father's story has seamlessly interwoven with our own, a source of strength and inspiration that will endure across generations to come. It is within this fusion of past and present, within this timeless narrative, that we find not an end but a new beginning.

This new beginning is adorned with the everlasting power of love, purpose, and the unyielding spirit of humanity. My father's legacy is an embodiment of the boundless possibilities that await when we summon the courage to follow the guidance of our hearts and dedicate ourselves to the betterment of our world.

As we embrace this new chapter, let it be known that my father's legacy is not confined to the pages of history but is alive in our actions, in the lives we touch, and in the difference we make. His legacy is powerful testament to the boundless possibilities that await when we follow our hearts and strive to make the world a better place for all.

End.

## Definition of terms

### Bayanihan

This term embodies the Filipino value of communal unity and working together for a common good. It is a community-driven process where support systems like family, friends, and community groups play a crucial role, especially in times of crisis and recovery.

### Kapampangan

Referring to the people of Pampanga, a province in the Philippines. In the book, they are depicted as resilient individuals, actively engaged in clearing debris and rebuilding their community after the eruption of Mount Pinatubo, demonstrating determination and collective strength.

### Lahar

Described in the book as a volcanic mudflow, more treacherous than lava flows. Lahar is a significant hazard following volcanic eruptions, as it involves the rapid flow of volcanic debris and water, capable of causing widespread destruction, particularly in the aftermath of the Pinatubo eruption.

### Mount Pinatubo

An active stratovolcano located on the island of Luzon in the Philippines. Its 1991 eruption, one of the largest volcanic eruptions of the 20th century, serves as a backdrop for the book. It is described as an ancient titan with a fiery heart, symbolizing both the natural beauty and the potential for destruction in nature.

## Sisig

A traditional Filipino dish, especially popular in Kapampangan cuisine. In the book, it symbolizes a sense of home, safety, and hope, and is part of a feast that celebrates survival and tradition.

## Temporary Shelter

In the context of the book, this refers to the makeshift accommodations provided for those displaced by the eruption of Mount Pinatubo. Described as immense spaces filled with families, these shelters were places of refuge, where laughter and conversations mingled, creating a symphony of resilience despite the challenges faced by the community.

**About the Author:**

Elaine Ayson, the daughter of a dedicated Army officer, embarked on a remarkable journey of resilience and compassion from a very young age. At the tender age of six, she bore witness to the catastrophic eruption of Mount Pinatubo, a natural disaster that left her entire hometown of Porac, Pampanga, in ruins. It was during this tumultuous period that the seeds of inspiration were sown, and Elaine's unwavering commitment to honor her father's lifelong service and commemorate the lives lost in the eruption began to take root.

Elaine's heartfelt dedication to producing this book is a testament to her boundless love and reverence for her father, who devoted the majority of his life to serving his fellow countrymen. His legacy of selflessness and dedication left an indelible mark on the author's heart, propelling her to share his story and the stories of countless others whose lives were forever changed by the eruption.

Through the pages of this book, Elaine invites us all to join her in celebrating the resilience of the human spirit and the countless capacity for compassion that resides within us. Her journey is a source of inspiration, reminding us that even in the face of unimaginable adversity, we have the power to rise, to heal, and to make a positive impact on the world.

As we embark on this empowering journey with Elaine, let us be inspired by her relentless determination to honor her father's legacy and pay tribute to the lives affected by the

Mount Pinatubo eruption. In her words and stories, we find a beacon of hope, a call to action, and a profound reminder that, together, we can make a difference in the lives of others and leave a lasting legacy of love and compassion.

Made in the USA
Las Vegas, NV
12 January 2024

84258685R00046